Teaching Kids Recorder

Teaching Kids Recorder

Margo Hall and Norma Kelsey

iUniverse, Inc.
New York Lincoln Shanghai

Teaching Kids Recorder

iUniverse books may be ordered through booksellers or by contacting:

iUniverse
2021 Pine Lake Road, Suite 100
Lincoln, NE 68512
www.iuniverse.com
1-800-Authors (1-800-288-4677)

ISBN-13: 978-0-595-36743-6 (pbk)
ISBN-13: 978-0-595-81163-2 (ebk)
ISBN-10: 0-595-36743-7 (pbk)
ISBN-10: 0-595-81163-9 (ebk)

Printed in the United States of America

We dedicate this book to our husbands,
John and Morrie,
and to our sons and their families
for their love and support

ACKNOWLEDGEMENTS

We are indebted to our families, colleagues and teachers for their inspiration. We are especially grateful to Renelle West for her editing expertise and encouragement, Tim Hall for his help with the photography, to Robert Fritz for teaching us the creative process, to Renelle West and Sanford Blum for cover photos, and to our friends in the Recorder Research Group: Barbara Biser, Rosanne Fraley, Jean Johnson, and Gail Jones.

CONTENTS

Introduction xi

Chapter One: K-2 Readiness for Recorder 1

Chapter Two: The Science of Sound 5

Chapter Three: Choosing Recorders 9

Chapter Four: Obtaining Recorders 12

Chapter Five: Classroom Organization 14

Chapter Six: The Path to Producing Beautiful Sounds 17

Chapter Seven: Adding to the One-Note Repertoire 24

Chapter Eight: Integrating the Recorder into Music Class Activities 31

Chapter Nine: Literacy 37

Chapter Ten: Assessment and Evaluation 41

Conclusion 43

Appendix A: Songs 45

Appendix B: Chants 47

Appendix C: Sample Letter to Parents 49

Resources 51

References 53

Biographies 55

INTRODUCTION

Our National Standards in music education advocate that all children learn to play an instrument. The recorder family has been played and enjoyed since medieval times. People still enjoy its warmth and beauty. The modern plastic recorder can sound beautiful. It is portable, inexpensive, and can provide a lifetime of enjoyment for relatively inexperienced as well as experienced players as a solo or ensemble instrument. For many children, the recorder can be the instrument they learn to play.

When each of us began to teach recorder, we had been teaching general/vocal music for nearly a decade. In all of our college training we did not learn to teach recorder to 30 squirmy children. The National Standards did not yet exist, but we wanted our students to be able to play an instrument. We looked for a good recorder method book. In our minds, the children would look at the book, find the note on the staff, find the right fingering, cover the holes, tap their foot on the floor to the steady beat, and play. With the right book, it couldn't be too difficult! But with each book we tried, it *was* too difficult. There was too much happening *all at once*. Maybe we just hadn't found the *right* book. If we could find the right book, then teaching recorder would be so much easier. It MUST exist somewhere, we thought.

After much searching, we found no such book. Recorder books we examined did not address our needs or the needs of the children. Some recorder method books even contradicted how we knew children best learn music. What we discovered was that before children open a recorder method book there is much learning that needs to take place, both physically and mentally. The task of playing the recorder must be broken down into small pieces, and we must prepare children for each piece of the task. The process of comprehending and performing music requires the building of schema, and none of the books addressed this process.

Teachers, too, need to build schema for teaching recorder. There is certain knowledge that teachers need before they can begin recorder instruction. Some teacher resources, such as books and workshops, are contradictory. Some are erroneous or incomplete. As we examined our knowledge about recorder teaching, we discovered that we held assumptions that were erroneous or incomplete. Do any of these assumptions belong to you?

- **Students learn to read music and learn to play recorder all at once.** Did you have to cook a gourmet meal the first time you stepped into the kitchen? Did you have to drive a stick shift on a highway the first time you drove? Was your first dance the tango? Did you learn to read and speak at the same time? Did you swim a hundred yards using the Australian crawl the first time you entered a pool?

- **Recorder playing shouldn't be taught, because it takes too much time away from singing.** Margo: "At first, we would work so hard trying to play recorder, we didn't sing the whole music period. Silly me. Singing is the foundation of musical experiences. Since my students couldn't all sing, I thought they could play instead and be satisfied. Wrong. They needed to sing, and recorder playing became an extension of the singing."

- **There's really nothing you can do to prepare students for the physical act of recorder playing. And who'd want to?** Norma: "The more I taught recorder, the more I discovered missing pieces to the physical puzzle of playing. If each "piece" could become automatic, it would ease their path to playing."

- **Thumb and finger placement is difficult to deal with in large classes.** Margo: "When a child played 'Jingle Bells' for me on the D pitch, her fingers thrashed wildly in the air to the beat of the song, half covering random holes. All I could discern was the rhythm of the song. Why did this child not understand how the air column works? I began to see that children need to understand the science of their instrument in order to understand the logic of fingering."

- **Make sure it's Baroque, not German.** Margo: "One year, after a friend's recommendation, I purchased German recorders for one of my third grade classes with school money. Now we could play F with as much ease as any other note. The song possibilities opened wide."

- **Buy a cheap recorder.** Norma: "I thought I was doing my school and parents a favor by saving money on inexpensive recorders. $2.00!!! The first class entered, two kids dropped their recorders on my *carpeted* floor, mouthpiece down (of course), and *crack*!!! The recorders were broken."

- **Teaching recorder is a classroom organization nightmare.** Norma: "I remember one of my first experiences with a class of first-time recorder players. It took so long to distribute the instruments, and then the fire alarm sounded. Between my inept organization and the fire drill, we lost the whole music period. Eventually I learned how to organize recorder time."

- **Tonguing is a mystery.** Norma: "I thought tonguing was such an easy concept. When my classes sounded like steam calliopes, I revised my thoughts and developed a method for teaching tonguing."

- **Recorder is a pre-band instrument. It's not much good for anything else.** Norma: "Some elementary band teachers told me this, and I believed them. They said it was really important that the kids read notes while playing an instrument *before* they joined the band. What the kids really need is a large repertoire of songs they can sing and play by ear. Playing by ear is readiness for reading notes. Children may not yet be reading notes fluently when they begin their first lessons on their band or orchestra instruments."

- **It's too hard! My melody bells are easier.** Melody bells are great for keyboard-type spatial experience, and for playing by ear or by rote. They are also good for children with physical handicaps that prevent them from playing the recorder. When children are ready to read music and play at the same time, the melody bells become a problem. It is very difficult for a child to play the bells while reading music. The bell player must look back and forth between printed music and bells, making it almost impossible to maintain the rhythm of the song.

- **Recorder playing for one term is enough for the students.** How well could children learn any of the following skills with only nine weeks of instruction, twice a week, for one year: multiplication tables, speaking French, reading words, playing violin, physical fitness, computer keyboarding?

- **There is a "best" recorder book.** Margo: "There certainly are some that are better than others. I found that the *best* recorder materials came directly from the music lessons I was teaching in my classroom."

- **Creating music is hard enough for students, so why do it on recorder?** Norma and Margo: "Children *can* create music for recorder, and so can teachers."

- **My students have been playing recorder for three years, and now the range of skills is so wide that some are bored, some are frustrated, and the rest are somewhere in between.** Norma and Margo: "We found ways to deal with this challenge!"

If you share any of the above assumptions, we think you will find this book helpful and enlightening. Through our own classroom research, we discovered how to integrate recorder into the three aspects of classroom music instruction: doing music (listening, performing, creating), becoming musically literate, and becoming knowledgeable about music. In this book we will show you how to prepare children for the physical aspects of recorder playing, how to plan for classroom management, and how to use recorders in the classroom as a natural component in lessons.

CHAPTER ONE

K-2 Readiness for Recorder

You can begin to prepare your students for recorder instruction on their very first day of music class. By engaging your first and second grade students in readiness activities, you are laying the foundation for future instruction on instruments that they will begin to learn to play in third grade. Third graders and older students with no previous readiness skills will also benefit from these activities. These readiness activities include singing, chanting, expressive movement, finger dexterity exercises, mirror and opposite orientation and music literacy skills.

Singing is the foundation of musical learning. Through *singing* activities, you can teach children to be able to *think songs in their heads.* Suggested singing activities include vocal exploration, echoing, call and response, and rote learning, all of which develop inner hearing. Ability to hear songs internally allows children to express music through their recorder and other instruments. It is important to refrain from singing with *your* students. Allowing them to sing without your voice, or other voices on tapes and CDs, gives them independence with melodic content. It is also important for the children to refrain from singing with you. They will better hear the quality and expression in your voice.

Simple songs we teach by rote in first and second grade that we later use for rote recorder repertoire include:

Hop Old Squirrel
What Kind of Shoes
Great Big Stars
Good News
Over My Head
Frog in the Meadow
Closet Key
Head and Shoulders, Baby
John the Rabbit
Skin and Bones

Hot Cross Buns
Oh, My, No More Pie
Turkey Song
This Little Light of Mine
Bow Wow Wow
Who Has the Penny?

We will explain later in the book how to use parts of these songs for playing.

Through *chants* children can learn to vocalize rhythm patterns. While chanting, they can learn to keep a steady beat on various parts of their bodies. These activities enable children to develop their own internal metronome. This ability leads to rhythmic playing of recorders. You will find some chants children enjoy in *Appendix B*. Chants and songs such as these can be found in many sources, including the music series books you are using in your classroom.

Expressive movement to music helps children hear melodic direction, form, phrasing, rhythm, dynamics, and other musical elements that apply to recorder playing. It can also afford an opportunity to develop some *finger dexterity*, learn to *mirror or oppose* teacher movements, and *draw in the air* to increase left and right side mobility. Developing these skills can contribute to their ability to learn to play recorder.

Finger dexterity exercises can be done while children are mirroring your movements. For example, use a recording of "Flight 76" (*Hooked on Classics* version of "Flight of the Bumblebee"). Children can mirror finger, hand, and body motions you invent to move with the music. The finger motions can involve various finger-to-thumb movements that will help improve finger dexterity. Performing these movements in the air, as your arm moves from one side to the other, can show phrasing.

The game of "Opposites" will help children  develop left/right orientation. Having the skill of positioning in opposition to you is important for recorder instruction, because you eventually will model recorder playing for your students. If they try to mirror your position, they will end up doing strange things with their recorders. If they learn the skill of positioning in opposition to you, instruction will be much easier. You can actually *finger your recorder correctly* while facing the class, instead of standing with your back to the class and holding the recorder upside down over your head or facing the students with your right hand at the top and your left at the bottom. The game of opposites takes very little time, and when repeated from time to time, the ability becomes automatic. Here is how you can do this activity:

1. Arrange the children in rows, standing, facing you (This does not work in a circle!), spread out with enough space to move their arms without bumping. Tell the children to mirror, or copy your movements. Make arm and hand motions on the left and right, alternating sides using one or both arms. You can accompany the movements with recorded music. When mirroring with music, use a variety of techniques, such as moving to the steady beat, using staccato as well as legato motions, turning the hands, and drawing in the air. Adjust the tempo of your movements to the ability of your students. Start with 16-beat patterns. When students are ready, increase the tempo and shorten the patterns to eight beats.

2. Stop and explain that when you say the word "opposites" they should use the opposite hand and arm, on the opposite side. Have them practice this skill without the music, then with music. Again, adjust the tempo and the number of beats per pattern to the ability of your students. Children with left/right orientation problems need to be positioned directly in front of you, not to the sides.

3. Combine the two concepts by calling the word "mirror" or the word "opposites" at random times as they copy your movements to the music.

Students can *draw in the air* their name, shapes, numbers, friends' names, and other objects with first one hand and then the other. You can also instruct them to draw in the air with their elbow, knee, ear, foot, nose, and head. Accompany this activity with various types of music that are contrasting in terms of dynamics, articulation, texture, pitch, or tempo. Vary the activity according to the form of the music. For example, use your upper body parts for the A section and lower body parts for the B section. You can devise a rondo with various body parts assigned to each section of the piece. Use your imagination and let your children use theirs.

By the end of second grade, students should be very familiar with basic tools of *music literacy*. They should be able to imitate, sing, play, write, and create with melodic and rhythmic solfege. They should be familiar with symbols such as quarter and eighth notes, the staff, treble clef sign, repeat sign, double bar, and some simple dynamic markings. They should have experience with both duple and triple meters.

Additionally, they should be able to perform automatically the following skills:

• Sing a number of songs independently

- Hear songs internally
- Move to a steady beat
- Move to rhythm patterns
- Move expressively to show various contrasts in music
- Demonstrate "mirror" and "opposite" movements
- Show finger dexterity

While you work to develop these skills with your students, you can also explore the science of sound.

CHAPTER TWO

The Science of Sound

It is important to explore the science of sound production and pitch change with your students. Combine basic facts about the science of sound with interesting hands-on activities. These activities will enable your children to understand how instruments work.

The first principle to understand is that **sound is vibration of air.** Sound cannot be seen, but the children can see and feel vibrations as they hear the sounds. The following activities will demonstrate this principle.

1. **Tuning fork in water:** Fill a bowl with water. Hit a tuning fork on a hard surface and immediately place the two tines of the fork in the water. The sound vibrations from the fork will send out waves of water from the tuning fork.

2. **Rubber band plucking:** Have one student hold a large rubber band, stretching it and holding it with tension. Have another student pluck the rubber band with his or her finger. Vibrations are visible.

3. **Plastic Ruler:** Hold a thin type of plastic ruler on a table or counter top so half of the ruler extends over the edge. When you pull down on the ruler and then let go, the ruler will vibrate and make sound. The vibrations will be easy to see.

4. **Drum vibrations:** Invite students to place their hands just inside the open end of a tubular-shaped drum, such as a conga drum. As you tap on the drumhead, the air inside the drum will vibrate, and the students will feel the vibrations hit their hands. A piece of thin paper held over the drum opening will move when the drum is struck, showing the force of the vibrations.

5. **String vibrations:** Strum all the strings of an autoharp slowly and then pluck them individually. Children will see the strings vibrating and hear the resulting sound. This string experiment can also lead to generalizations about the effect of size on pitch. It is important for children to

understand that **pitch is determined by size,** whether it is a drumhead, a string, a metal bar, or a column of air. When children cover holes on their recorders, they will be changing the size of the air column contained in the body of the recorder.

Before beginning the following demonstrations, discuss the difference between pitch and volume. Stress the use of the terms "high" and "low" for pitch only, and "loud" and "soft" for volume.

1. **Autoharps:** Children can take turns plucking the strings, one at a time, from large to small, or the other way around, generalizing about the effect of string length and thickness on pitch.

2. **Melody bells or xylophone:** Children can see the difference in bar size and generalize about pitch difference.

3. **Set of triangles of various sizes:** Children can explore pitch and size relationship.

4. **Water glasses of the same size:** Children can compare the effect of differing amounts of water on pitch.

5. **Hand drums of varying sizes:** Children can compare pitches.

6. **Panpipes:** Play a simple and familiar song. Next, play a scale from highest to lowest pitch. Ask the children which of the pipes had higher pitches and which had lower pitches.

If children have ever tried to make sound on a tube of air, they may wonder how to get the air to vibrate to produce a sound. Insert one of the panpipe tubes directly into your mouth and blow, demonstrating that no sound can be produced this way. Now, get the air to vibrate by blowing the stream of air so that it splits on the edge of the panpipe. The panpipe demonstration can lead to discussion about another principle of sound: **splitting an air column produces sound.** You can explain why you are blowing your column of air across the pipe opening so that about half goes over the edge and about half goes down the tube. Show how to do this on a soda pop bottle. Children can then try the experiment at home. They can try different sizes of bottles and different levels of water in the bottles to generalize about size and pitch.

Explain that panpipes evolved into flutelike instruments. Compare the panpipes with a fife or transverse flute. Play a scale on both the panpipes and the flute for the children and give them an opportunity to discuss the main difference, that *one "pipe"* now replaces a set of pipes.

Compare the panpipes with a recorder. Play a scale on each for the children and give them an opportunity to discover two ways the instruments are different: On the recorder, *one "pipe"* replaces a set of pipes. In addition, on the recorder, there is a *built-in device that splits the air,* so that about half of the air goes down the tube and half goes out the window (see illustration). It is important for the children to understand how the column of air is changing lengths, and thus pitches, as you cover the holes from top to bottom.

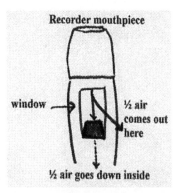

If you ask children where half of the air exits the instrument, many will answer that it exits at the bottom. Ask the children to hold a hand under the bottom while you play. The child will feel just a little air moving. Ask the child to hold a hand near the holes on the front of the instrument as you play. The child will feel air moving through the first open hole near the top. Cover the holes from top to bottom, one at a time. Play a note each time, and ask the children to predict what will happen to the pitch, and where the air will exit. This demonstration will show that **the larger the air column, the lower the pitch.**

Where does the sound itself come out of a recorder? Your students may ask this question. The best way to demonstrate the answer is with a microphone. Use a real microphone or one from the dollar store. A student can hold the microphone in various places around the instrument as you play. The children will discover that the sound comes out the window of the recorder.

Why do higher, "squeaky" pitches sometimes happen? This is an important question because children tend to overblow at first, producing high squeals on their recorders. While these are real pitches, they are not usually desirable. Produce some high squeals on your recorder intentionally and ask the children if they know how to fix this problem. A discussion will lead to the conclusion that by vibrating a column of air more rapidly, higher pitches will be produced. Conversely, a slower speed of air will produce lower pitches.

In this chapter, you read about some important principles of sound that will impact recorder playing:

- **Sound is vibration of air**
- **Pitch is determined by size**
- **Splitting an air column produces sound**
- **The larger the air column, the lower the pitch**
- **Speed of air can determine pitch**

By experiencing the principles of sound production, your students will be able to understand why they need to cover holes properly, and why fingering makes sense. They are ready to experience sound production on recorders.

CHAPTER THREE

Choosing Recorders

During third grade, children can begin actual playing. Now you must decide which recorders and other supplies to buy. You can purchase recorders at a local music store or through music supply catalogs.

German vs. Baroque (English) Fingering

There are two types of soprano recorders: Baroque and German. Baroque recorders require a difficult finger manipulation for the F note that most elementary kids can't manage. Teachers using Baroque recorders compensate for this by avoiding songs with F, which eliminates a lot of enjoyable and important repertoire. The Baroque recorder has remained in use because many musicians believe the intonation is superior to that of German recorders, but we have found German recorders with good intonation, such as Aulos, Yamaha, and Peripole. We believe that recorders with German fingering are best for beginners.

Plastic vs. Wood

The real purists who play recorders professionally will perform on wooden recorders, but will practice on plastic recorders. Children do not need good wooden recorders. Wooden recorders do not perform well when they are damp, and children tend to chew on the mouthpiece and use more saliva than necessary. Intonation is a problem with inexpensive wooden instruments; in fact it's a problem with expensive ones, too. There is also the increased risk of the instrument breaking. In short, we believe that plastic recorders of a reputable brand are just fine for young beginners.

How Many Pieces?

Recorders come in one-, two-, and three-piece models. While two- and three-piece models are more tunable and adjustable, they are also a huge distraction for young beginners. Mouthpieces end up backwards, and foot pieces end up lost. We heartily recommend one-piece models.

Thumb Guide or Not?

Some recorders come with a plastic protrusion on the lower back side just above the location for the right thumb. The purpose of this thumb guide is to

ensure that the player will have proper placement of the thumb. This will enable proper alignment of the hands and fingers resulting in better speed and accuracy. This is particularly beneficial for young students. We have found that when young students feel the thumb guide above their thumb, they are more likely to keep their thumb there when only the left hand fingers are moving. High D is an example of a note for which right thumb placement is crucial. There are some minor drawbacks to this permanently placed thumb guide:

- Not all hands are created equal in size, so actual thumb placement differs slightly among players.
- Children will sometimes use the thumb guide as a handle or place their thumb above the guide instead of below it. Imagine the contortions!

We feel that the benefits of permanent thumb guides outweigh the drawbacks.

There are several other types of thumb guides. We have seen moveable plastic guides that snap onto the recorder. One can only imagine where these will actually end up! There are also circular Velcro spots that the teacher sticks onto the recorder according to each child's individual thumb placement. The child is supposed to feel the spot and put his/her thumb there, on the spot. These, too, end up in interesting places, because they peel off easily. Both of these methods are time consuming for the teacher.

Note: While some manufacturers refer to this thumb piece as a thumb rest, we prefer to call it a guide, because some students think their thumb should rest on top of it, when the thumb actually goes below it.

Lanyards

It is convenient to attach one's recorder to a lanyard. We wear our recorder on a lanyard when we are teaching so that we don't have to look for it every time we want to use it. When the children wear their recorders, they can easily make transitions among activities without losing track of their recorders. When children perform they can combine the activities of singing and recorder playing without the messy procedure of distributing and collecting instruments on stage, and without the worry of dropping recorders on the floor.

Some manufacturers provide a lanyard with each recorder, consisting of a rope and a ring that slips around the bottom of the recorder and slides up past the finger holes. While the idea is appealing, know that lanyards can be made quite easily with ribbon and a small, thin 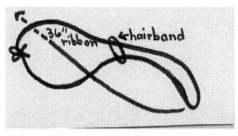 elastic hair band (see illustration). Other considerations are far more important when choosing a recorder.

Brand

With a changing and competitive industry, manufacturers are striving to develop quality recorders at a reasonable price. We recommend that you buy and try various brands before you purchase recorders for your students. Compare recorders for quality of sound, ease of obtaining sound on low C, and intonation. Check for durability. Drop a recorder, mouthpiece downward, on a hard floor, and see what happens! Run it through the dishwasher and see what happens! Be forewarned that some very cheap brands of recorders, available at bargain stores, may vary in pitch from the standard A=440 by as much as a quarter or half tone. Tell any child with such a recorder that he/she can use it at home, but it won't work in a group.

Once you have decided which recorders to purchase, you are ready to explore how to obtain them.

CHAPTER FOUR

Obtaining Recorders

Ideally, it would be great for the students to have one recorder at school and one at home. Children can then practice at home the skills they learn at school. They can share their successes with their family and friends. They can get together with friends and play. They will always have a recorder at school to play. Their school recorder won't get lost on the bus, dropped in the parking lot, or be forgotten at home. The dog won't chew it!

How can you accomplish this ideal in your school? You can issue each child a recorder for the year, to be kept at school, and the parents can purchase a recorder for the child to play at home.

School-owned recorders can be sanitized in a dishwasher with detergent and bleach at the end of the school year, and be re-issued the following school year.

What if your budget is too small to purchase enough recorders for all of your students who are learning to play? Emphasize the benefits of recorder instruction within your music program to your principal, the parents, the children, and organizations. The National Standards include a directive that all children should learn to play an instrument.

If necessary, try to find an organization that is willing to donate the recorders. Another option is to gradually build up your school-owned supply by purchasing some recorders each year.

Child-owned recorders can be purchased through a school store, the P.T.A., or you, the music teacher. Some schools require children to purchase them as part of their school supplies. Find out from your principal how to add the recorder to the required school supply list. Send a letter to the parents explaining details about recorder purchase. (See Appendix C for a sample letter.) Most parents are willing to pay less than $10 for an instrument that will be used at least three years.

Sometimes the PTA will handle selling recorders for the music teacher. You can contact a local music store, order the required number of recorders, and the P.T.A. will pay for them and sell them to students. Arrange with the store manager for unsold recorders to be returned. If the number of unsold recorders is small, perhaps these could be donated to needy students.

What if some students cannot afford to purchase their own recorders? Speak with your principal about the situation. Ask for permission to find an organization, such as the P.T.A., or other civic organization, that would be willing to donate recorders to children. The principal can help you determine which children would need this donation. This donation would have to be handled in the strictest confidence to protect the privacy of the families involved. If many children are in need, perhaps an organization would donate recorders to all children in the grade levels in which you are teaching recorder.

What if the ideal is not attainable? It is not always possible for every child to have a recorder available at school as well as one at home. Perhaps you are trying to gradually build up your supply at school, and have not attained enough recorders for everyone. In this case, require children to purchase a recorder and keep it at school. Children can then take them home for holiday breaks and for the summer, remembering to bring them back afterward.As an alternative, children can keep their recorder in their backpack, removing it at home to practice, and at school for music class.

There will be some children who do not purchase a recorder for one reason or another. Issue a school-owned recorder to these children for the year, and keep them at school, or arrange for a donation from an organization.

Putting stick-shaped noisemakers in the hands of 30 nine and ten year olds can be a frightening prospect. How will you plan for storage, distribution, safety, hygiene, and manners? In the next chapter, you will find some answers.

CHAPTER FIVE

Classroom Organization

Before distributing recorders the first time, it will be important to establish rules for safety, hygiene, and good manners.

Safety

Issues of safety are serious. Discuss the importance of safety. Deal with them firmly and immediately. Be watchful. Discuss rules again when necessary. Children need to be reminded of the importance of the rules, and they need to know you mean to enforce them. You may need to hold a child's recorder for a while during the class and return it to the child when he assures you that he is ready to follow the rules and understands their importance. We consider the following rules to be essential, based on our own experience:

- Children should be as still as possible and stay in their own space when they have recorders in their mouths, in order to avoid hurting their mouths and damaging their teeth.
- They should not touch other children who have recorders in their mouths.
- A child should not blow a recorder in another child's ear.
- Children should not use their recorders to touch other children.

Hygiene

Hygiene issues can be as serious as safety issues. Diseases such as hepatitis and AIDS make the sharing of instruments dangerous. Children must understand that they should ***never place another child's instrument in their mouth.*** If a child accidentally does place another child's recorder in his or her mouth, the recorder should be sanitized by soaking the mouthpiece in a solution of one part bleach to nine parts water for ten minutes, rinsed thoroughly, and allowed to air dry.

Manners

Discuss why it is important to have manners. Help children imagine the chaos that would result from everyone playing when they feel like it. At home in their own room, it would not matter, but in a crowd of 20 or 30 children, the class would accomplish little if they had to wait for one person to choose to stop playing. Again, holding a child's recorder for a while can be effective. *Children should play only when instructed to do so.*

Storing and Distributing

Small fingering charts usually come with recorders. These are useless for young beginners. They are printed on thin paper, folded too many times, and difficult for children to interpret. If they came with school-owned recorders, throw them away. If they came with student-owned recorders, tell the children to take the charts home so that they do not end up stuffed in the bottom of the plastic case, or on the floor of your classroom. Tell the children to put their chart in a safe place; for example, in their sock drawer. This way they can always find it when they become advanced enough to make use of it.

In addition to the charts, the students will usually find useless swab sticks. These are plastic sticks with a hole in one end, to which the student is supposed to knot one end of a small rag to dry the inside of the recorder. It doesn't work. Recorders do get damp on the inside when they are played. If sufficient moisture builds up, it can interfere with the airway, and there will be no sound. It is unlikely that this will happen to beginners, because they will probably not play long enough for so much moisture to collect. If they are school-owned recorders, collect the sticks and dispose of them. If they are student-owned, they can go in the sock drawer with the fingering chart. There are some recorder swabs available for purchase that will work.

If you keep your students' recorders at school, store the recorders for each class in a separate, labeled dishpan. Store them individually in their cases, in plastic bags, or socks labeled with their names. Socks work well, because the children recognize their own sock, and the damp recorder can dry out better in a sock after each use.

Develop a routine with each class so that children know whose responsibility it is to distribute and collect recorders. When you greet your class in the hallway before they enter your classroom, instruct the designated helpers to distribute recorders. Each class should have a specific place for its dishpan. Have a plan for where children will put their recorder, still in its case or sock, when they receive it. For example, they might place it under their chair or in their lap. If the children have lanyards, they should put them on when you direct them to do so.

The children should now be ready for their first lesson.

CHAPTER SIX

The Path to Producing Beautiful Sounds

Now the children are ready to pick up their recorders. This won't be a scary moment, because in this chapter you will learn just what to do.

You are wearing your recorder on a lanyard around your neck, the same model the children will be playing. It is important that you use the same recorder model, so that the children will hear the quality of sound for which they are aiming. We know from our own experience that children will notice the difference in sound and will try to match the teacher's sound. If your recorder is different, like a wooden one that is naturally louder, the children will be unable to match your sound, and they will have intonation problems and experience frustration.

Modeling tone is an important component of learning. Play a familiar tune, such as "Michael, Row the Boat Ashore" for the class from memory. You are modeling the beauty of the recorder as a musical instrument.

The children will be anxious to play. Taking time to establish a foundation in the fundamentals of playing will pay big dividends. The following procedures can be accomplished in a short period of time and are well worth the effort.

Holding the Instruments

Tell the children to pick up their recorders and remove them from the cases, which can then be stored under their chairs. If the children have lanyards, show them how to put the lanyards on the recorders and wear them.

For just a few moments, stand with your back to the children, looking over

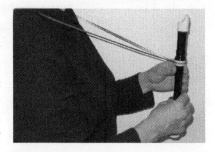

your shoulder, of course! Hold your instrument vertically, high in the air, so that the children can see that your left hand is on top, with thumb and first finger in "B" position. Keep your fingers flat, but relaxed.

Tell the children to follow these directions:

1. Hold the recorder a comfortable distance away from their chest with the mouthpiece pointing to the ceiling, and the back of the recorder (where there is only one hole) facing them.

2. Put the left hand near the top and put the left thumb over the hole that they can see. At this time there will probably be at least one child who will want to place his or her right hand at the top, and will complain about using the left hand. This complaint will surface again—be assured! Here is a way to deal with handedness. Say: "Your right hand has a really tough job to do at the bottom of your recorder. Your left hand has easier stuff to do right now, at the top."

3. *Without looking*, let the left pointer finger find and cover the hole opposite the thumb, on the front side. *Why not look?* In order to play a recorder, one must be able to place one's fingers on desired holes without stopping to look for the holes. Imagine what would happen if *clarinet* players had to stop and look at their hands every time they needed to move a finger! Children *will* try to do this. Moving the recorder to look at the fingers disrupts the hand position, often creating air leaks, and disrupts the rhythm of the song.

4. Place the right thumb below the thumb guide. If there is no thumb guide, follow these steps:

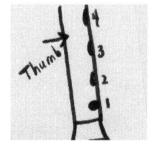

   a. Look at the front of the recorder and count up 3 holes from the bottom.

   b. Place your thumb on the back side behind the space between holes 3 and 4. (*See picture.*)

Turn to face the students. Tell the children that now they will be doing "opposites" with you.

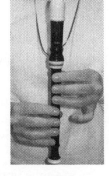

Fat Pads

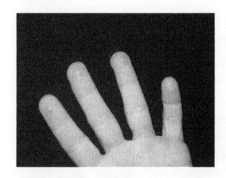

It is important to show the children the difference between the fingertips and the "fat pads" of their fingers. Fat pads are the fleshy parts *near* the fingertips, but not the tips themselves. Ask the children which of the two parts of their finger is bigger and softer and would seal up the hole better so no air could escape. Using the fat pads will enable them to completely cover the holes, while inserting the fingertips into the holes will result in air leaks. Emphasize that the fat pads should be snuggled into the holes covered by their first finger and thumb, in order to produce their first sound. The children can check for "fat pad" coverage by looking at their fingers to see if there are little circles where each fat pad pushed into the hole. (We tell the children not to worry about the circles on their fingers. "They will go away by the time you get married.") This technique works well for all finger combinations. If you do not address this issue in advance, some children will try to curve their fingers and cover the holes with their fingertips. **Curled fingers, as in piano position, do not work for recorder playing** (see photo). Children become frustrated when every pitch they try to produce with varied fingering sounds like "D."

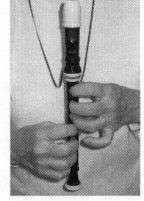

Total Hand Position

Use this sequence of steps to begin your instruction each time the class meets, until the skills become automatic. Repetition builds automaticity, or the ability of the body and brain to perform a task automatically.

1. Position the recorder with the mouthpiece resting on their <u>chin</u> just below their lower lip. This is called "chin position."

2. Begin to add fingers, one at a time until all fingers of both hands are in position.

3. Snuggle the fat pads on their fingers into the holes.

4. If there is a thumb guide, put the right thumb <u>below</u> it, not above it.

5. If the bottom two holes are double-holed, treat the doubles as a single hole and cover both holes with the one finger.

6. Remove one hand and put it back, then the other hand. It is important to emphasize that the right thumb must stay "at home" and not go away "on vacation." Sometimes the students will feel that the right hand is not needed if it is not covering any holes, but it is needed for balance.

7. Check the recorder's balance by holding the recorder in chin position with only the right thumb below the thumbguide. If there is no thumb guide, check the balance by lifting all fingers except the right thumb and the left middle finger.

8. Let their fingers "hang out" over the holes. Another possible image might be: "Pretend your fingers are helicopters hovering over the landing pad."

9. After all fingers are down, lift all fingers, except for the right thumb and the left hand "B" finger and thumb, just enough to *hover* slightly above the holes.

Keeping the fingers close to the holes is important, in order to have the fingers ready to cover the holes at a moment's notice. Call for a "finger drill" at any time the children have recorders, expecting them to instantly place their fingers on the holes. This can be a humorous challenge, and it also keeps them aware of the importance of fingers hovering near the holes. Use any image you can give your students to accomplish the task.

Rest Position

Play the "opposite game" by holding and turning your recorder in various positions. End this short exercise in rest position with the "B" still fingered with the left hand, and the recorder lying across the lap, the mouthpiece facing the left, the right hand resting on top of the lower part of the recorder. If children are using lanyards, they can let the recorders hang against their chests and put their hands in their laps. Tell the children this is called "**rest position.**" Have them maintain the rest position while you demonstrate tonguing.

Tonguing

Tell the children to listen closely as you play two different ways. Play a short phrase with tonguing and then the same phrase without tonguing. Ask the children to describe the difference in what they hear. You may have to do this several times. When the children can hear and describe the difference, show them, without your recorder, what you are doing. Gently whisper the word "took" without the "k." Make sure the "t" is not explosive, but closer to a "d" as in the word "photo." If you model the "t" correctly, the students will understand the subtle difference. Of course, there are no guarantees that they will do it! These four steps will enable children to tongue properly:

1. With recorder in <u>chin position</u>, not in the mouth, gently say a short rhythm pattern using the syllable "too," such as:

2. Invite the children to imitate.

3. Slide recorder onto lower lip. Again demonstrate gentle tonguing using a pattern and invite the children to imitate.

4. With recorder on lower lip, feel and seal your lips (no teeth!) around the tip of the mouthpiece, and demonstrate gentle tonguing using a pattern. Invite the children to imitate. Now the children are actually producing a sound on their recorder. Ta-da!!!!!!!

Allow children to shake out their hands and return their recorder to rest position in order to learn about breathing.

Breathing: "I'll huff and I'll puff and I'll blow..."

This is the normal inclination of children! Model the breathing of a gentle, slow and sustained column of air into the recorder. Several images may help. The image of a candle works well. Hold your index finger up in the air as if it were a candle with a flame on top. Pretend to blow out the flame as if it were a birthday candle. Then, gently, slowly blow a small stream of air, pretending to make the flame flicker without extinguishing it. Ask: "Which one would work better for the recorder?" Repeat the gentle, sustained blowing while the children time you to see how long you can sustain your breath. The children can then gently blow while you time them.

Another image for helping the children to control their breath: Hold your hand flat about four inches from your face and huff gently on it as you would to create a fog on a car window when it's raining.

Rhythm Patterns on "B"

Play four-beat patterns for the children to echo, reminding them to tongue and breathe gently. After a few minutes, go to this pattern:

This leads to the first song, *Hop Old Squirrel*, which the children learned to sing previously.

Playing Our First Song

1. **Sing *Hop Old Squirrel*.** While the children maintain rest position with their recorders, review the singing of "Hop Old Squirrel."

2. **Tongue and Sing *Hop Old Squirrel*.** With recorders in chin position, while fingering a B, tell the children to sing the song in the following manner, substituting all the "hop old squirrel" words with the "too" sound on the B pitch:

   > Too, too, too, eidle dum eidle dum, (pronounced *eye-dl-dum*)
   > Too, too, too, eidle dum dum.
   > Too, too, too, eidle dum eidle dum,
   > Too, too, too, eidle dum dee.

3. Play and Sing "Hop Old Squirrel"

Now, slip the recorder into the mouth for the "toos" and slip it back out to sing the "eidle dums."

Your first lesson was a success! Your students can play "B" as "mi" and incorporate it into a song they are singing. They can't wait to play again, and you aren't dreading lesson #2.

CHAPTER SEVEN

Adding to the One-Note Repertoire

Warm up

Now that you have laid the groundwork, you can begin each lesson with a routine of warm-ups. Design your warm-ups to review the skills that need to be reinforced so that they become automatic. When previously learned skills become automatic, the children can attend to and manage a new task more successfully.

Use expressive movement warm-ups to recorded music beginning with large movements, and progressing to finger dexterity exercises to the steady beat. (See Chapter One.)

Review mirroring/opposite skills, breathing, tonguing, posture, hole coverage, and hand position. Children will engage more productively if warm-ups consist of more "doing" and less "talking" by the teacher.

Use a "Recorder Reminders" chart to help the children self-check. The chart could include items such as:

- *Left hand* on top, right hand on the bottom
- *Tongue* every note
- *Musicians' posture*
- Warm, foggy, gentle *breath*
- *Snuggle* the fingers into the holes
- Fingers *hang out* over the open holes

As the children learn new notes, add finger exercises to the warm-up routine. We like to call these "calisthenics." (It is always good to use physical education terminology. Kids understand the connection.)

Here is how we do "calisthenics":

1. Place the recorder in chin position and ask the students to do the same.
2. Ask them to place fingers in "B" position.

3. Add the next finger down, covering the hole well enough that we can hear a "pop."

4. Practice lifting and replacing that finger several times.

5. This new note is called "A."

Use the calisthenics to practice the finger positions of any pitches and combinations of pitches that the children will be playing that day. Some pitch combinations are trickier than others. For example, when playing "B" to "G," tell the children to think about their middle finger and ring finger as a team that must go up and down at the same time. If there are still a few children who play "A" on the way to "G," suggest to them that they think of putting down the ring finger before the middle finger. This usually solves the problem.

After doing calisthenics in the chin position, let the children echo your long tones and rhythm patterns on "B" and on any other notes you have taught. It is much easier to start at "B" and add fingers one at a time than it is to start on a lower pitch that uses more than two fingers. For that reason we always start our warm-ups on "B." Gradually the children will be able to play all the way down to low "C" using long tones, adding one finger at a time.

Play in tune together

Long tones are a great opportunity for children to practice listening in order to play in tune together. You will hear as many variations on the pitch as there are children playing! It is important to teach children to listen for and match the correct pitch. One way to do this is to demonstrate pitch matching with a keyboard pitch.

Play a sustained "B" on a keyboard. Then, play a sustained "B" on the recorder. Vary the pitch of your recorder by over-blowing and under-blowing the "B." Keep altering the recorder pitch above and below "B" on the keyboard, bringing the recorder pitch gradually into synchronization with the keyboard pitch. As you do this exercise again, ask the children to raise their hands when the pitch of the recorder matches the pitch of the keyboard. Hold the pitch there, and then depart again from the actual pitch. The children will hear the change and will lower their hands when the recorder pitch departs from that of the keyboard. Do this several times until the children can hear exactly when the two pitches match. Ask them to explain how you did that, since it is obvious that you didn't change anything with your fingers. They should conclude that you were breathing faster and slower to change the pitch.

Ask the children to play "B" together, sustaining and adjusting the speed of their breath until all are playing the same pitch, in tune. This really works! Children really can learn to listen to pitch as they play.

After children can play B, A, G, and low E, we use a C major scale as a beautiful warm-up, using long tones in order to encourage children to listen to the intonation, and to blend their tones together. The slow pace of the scale and the order of fingering also ease the ability of the children to play tones that require more fingers. Start on B, and when the tones all match, indicate to the children to add the next finger down, then the next, and so forth. When you arrive at low C, pick up fingers one at a time until you arrive back at B. At this point, flip the fingers to arrive at high C. Eventually, you can add high D, and then settle back on high C. A beautiful chordal accompaniment on the keyboard adds to the beauty of the song. Remind the children to keep their right thumb in place as the fingers on the right hand all lift.

Play parts of songs by rote

Just as the children learned to play "Hop Old Squirrel" in the key of "G" using "B," they can now play it in the key of "F" using "A." They can then play it in the key of E-flat using G. You could accompany them on the keyboard in those keys. Remember, the children play their one pitch for the words, "Hop old squirrel," and sing the other words.

If your students need more work on "B," "A," and "G" separately, "Hop Old Squirrel" can have some adventures. You can make up additional verses, changing the tempo of the song to match the story. Old Squirrel can run, chase, row, climb, cycle, jog, etc. In between verses, you can spin a yarn about where he was going and why. Invite the children to enhance the story. We've had Old Squirrel on trips, getting chased by a dog, getting married, and even getting run over by a car (minor key!).

This sing-and-play technique works for dozens of songs. Children should be able to sing the song independently before combining the singing with recorder playing. Here are several songs that we use in the beginning stages. Prepare students for playing the fingering changes with their recorders in chin position. Have the students vocalize the sound "too" as in "took" to the rhythm pattern of the song as they finger the pitches.

Song Title	Key	Pitches	Words Played	Preparation
Good News	G	B, B to A	*Good news*	B to A
Good News	F	A, A to G	*Good news*	A to G
Good News	E flat	G, G to F	*Good news*	G to F
Head and Shoulders, Baby	F or G	F or G	*One, two, three*	F or G
What Kind of Shoes	G	B, A, B	*What kind of shoes you gonna wear?*	B to A, then quickly back to B
Great Big Stars	G	G, A	*Great big stars*	G and A long tones
Over My Head	G	G to B, G to A	*Over my head*	G to B, G to A
Trot, Old Joe	G	B, G, G	*Trot, old Joe*	B to G, repeat G
Who's Got a Fish-pole?	G	G to B to G	*Who's got a fish-pole?*	G to B to G
There She Goes	G	G, B, G G, A, B, A, G	*There she goes* the remaining words	G to B, then quickly back to G
Closet Key	G	G to B and G,B,A,B	First phrase and second phrase	G to B G,B,A,B
Bow, Bow, Wow	G	G to B B, A, G	*Bow, wow, wow* on G, *Whose dog art thou* on B. Last *Bow, wow, wow* on B, A, G	Three G's Three B's B to A to G
Frog in the Meadow	G	B, A, G	Any phrase	Pitches of the chosen phrase
Fais Do Do	G	B, A, G	*Fais do do*	B, A, G
Hot Cross Buns	G	B, A, G	*All the words*	B, A, G, A, B
John the Rabbit	E min	E	*Oh, yes!*	Play long tones on B, A, G, E
Skin and Bones	E min	B, A, G, E, Tongue B, slur A,G,E	*oo-oo-oo-ooh*	Sing "ooh" passage on B, A, G and E while fingering
Hot Cross Buns	G	B, A, G	*Hot cross buns!*	B to A to G
Hot Cross Buns	F	A, G, F	*Hot cross buns!*	A to G to F
Who Has the Penny?	F	C, A, C C, A, F	*Who has the penny?* *Who has the pin?*	C to A to C C to A to F
Oh My, No More Pie	Em	B, G, E	Echo the words	B to G to E
Turkey Song	Em	BBB, A, G, E, D, E	*And his feet were mighty dirty*	B,A,G,E,D,E, Tonguing the mel. rhythm on "Too" while singing, same while fingering

Song Title	Key	Pitches	Words Played	Preparation
Rattlin' Bog	G	BBAGEE	*Oh, row, the rattlin' bog*	Sing mel. as you tongue on too, same w/fingering
This Little Light of Mine	G	DDDD,E,G, BBBB,A,G	*This little light of mine, I'm gonna let it shine*	Pentachord, D,E, G, A, B
Swapping Song	G	EEDEGG, GABBBA	Refrain: *To my wing wong waddle, to my jack straw straddle,*	Pentachord, D, E, G, A, B

You can change the keys of these songs in order to add other fingerings you are teaching. There is a great advantage in using songs the children already know and can play.

Play entire songs that are based on the pentachord.

When your students can play up and down the D-E-G-A-B-D' pentachord, they will be able to play many songs. Eventually, you will be able to add high E to this pentachord. Students can find high E from high D simply by adding the third finger.

The F Pentachord also works with many songs: middle C-D-F-G-A-C'-D.' Remember, children need to be able to sing the songs independently before attempting to play them. Also, the children can sing some parts and play other parts of a song before playing the whole song.

The following is a list of pentachord-based songs:

Ahrirang
All Night, All Day
Ezekial Saw de Wheel
I Got a Robe
Indian Game Song (Uni Nuni)
Land of the Silver Birch
Little David
Mister Fron Went A-Courtin'
Night Herding Song
Oh, Won't You Sit Down
Old Brass Wagon
Old Dan Tucker
Old MacDonald
Old Texas
Rattlin' Bog
Sailing at High Tide
Seminole Duck Dance

Sourwood Mountain
Swapping Song
Swing Low, Sweet Chariot
The Angel Band
The Fish Pole Song
The Lone Star Trail
This Little Light
Turn the Glasses Over
Wayfaring Stranger

Play Popular Music

Play popular songs with or without CD accompaniment. Use the recording if the key is right. Explore the use of karaoke recordings. Perhaps children can sing some parts and play other parts of the song. Accompany children on a keyboard. Here are a few of our favorites:

We Will Rock You, key of a minor
Wim O Weh, key of C
Winter Wonderland, key of C
YMCA
One Note Samba, key of B flat

While exploring a popular dance CD by Christy Lane, we found that parts of the following songs will work on recorder:

Bunny Hop
Twist
Hustle
Hot, Hot, Hot
Chicken Dance
Hokey Pokey

The Importance of Rote Playing

Playing by rote, as in the above activities, builds strong musicianship without the burden of note reading. Do it often. We learn to be musicians in the same way we learn our language: by rote. Shinichi Suzuki called this "the mother tongue" method (Suzuki, p. 10). "Music is for the ear, not the eye, and therefore should be experienced thoroughly and consciously before its symbols are introduced." (Mills, p. 155)

Incorporate the echoing of tonal patterns and rhythm patterns into your warm-ups. Expand the children's repertoire from parts of songs to whole songs. Integrate rote recorder playing with other music class activities. The next chapter will show you how to do this.

CHAPTER EIGHT

Integrating the Recorder into Music Class Activities

You have taught the children in your classroom to sing a number of songs they can use for recorder playing. There are many ways in which you can build on this foundation, using songs that they have learned in their music series books or other resources. Once the children are able to sing these songs independently they are ready to play them on their recorders, play instruments with them, move to them, and create other songs. Here are some ideas for integrating singing and playing.

Sing and play

One group of children can sing the song while the others play part or all of the song. Here are some examples, in order of difficulty:

1. "Who's Got a Fish Pole?" is a song in which the question can be played on the recorder by one half of the class, and the answer can be sung by the other half of the class.
2. "Oh My, No More Pie" is an echo song. Some students can sing the verse, and others can play the echo.
3. "Charlie Over the Ocean" requires two melodic patterns. The first phrase, in the key of G, uses G, A and B. The second phrase uses G, E and D.
4. Advanced players can echo singers in the song, "Old Texas" in the key of F. They only need C, D, F, G, A, and high C and D.

You or the children can find a part in a round or other song that can become an ostinato. Some children can play the ostinato on the recorder while other children sing. Here are some examples that work well:

Title of song	Key	Ostinato Part
Banuwa	C	Any phrase
Bow Wow Wow	Any	Any phrase
Canoe Song	E min	Phrase I, BAGE
Christmas is Coming	D or C	Christmas is Coming
Come and Sing Together	D min	Meas. 2: FGFED
Debka Hora	D minor	Measures 5-8
Frere Jacques	F, G	FCF or GDG as in "Ding Dong Ding"
Hey, Ho, Nobody Home	G min	Phrase I, GFGD
Hinay Mah Tov	D min	Part I: DGFEDEFED
I Love the Mountains	F	Boom-dee-ah-da: FEDGC
Kookaburra	C	Phrases 1, 2, or 4
Little Tommy Tinker	C	Last phrase: E DC
Oh, How Lovely Is the Evening	Any	Tonic/Doh on the "Ding Dong"
Ooni Nooni	C	Phrases 1, 2, 4 Play E,G pattern
Row, Row, Row Your Boat	C	Phrase 1: CDE
Sandy McNab	F, G	Third phrase CF or DG
Scotland's Burning	F, G	Any phrase
Sing Together	F	Last phrase: CFCF
Sweetly Sings the Donkey	C, D, E, F, G	Hee-Haw: GC or AD,etc.
The Clock	C	Sing phrase 1, play the rest
The Frog	F, G	Last part, High C, low C, F
The Orchestra	C	The horn, drum, and clarinet parts
The Swan Sings	C	Bar 1 and/or bar 4
Three Blind Mice	C	Phrase 1: EDC and/or Phrase 2: GFE
Tick Tock	D	Phrase 1: DF-sharp
Turkish Rally Song	D min	The chant phrase on D
Where is John?	C, D	Last part, C or D
White Sand and Gray Sand	F	Part 1: FGFEF
Zum Gali Gali	F min or G min	Meas. 2: FFFCF or GGGDG

Children can play entire rounds. The song, "Snail, Snail," can be sung and played as a two-part round. Divide the class into two groups. Have group one sing the song, and have group two play, beginning when group one arrives at the second measure. Another way to use this song is to have both groups sing the first time through, play the second time, and sing the third time in a round. "Bow Wow Wow," "Scotland's Burning" and "Banuwa" can be played in their entirety in a round, alternating with singing.

Some songs have partner songs. These are songs that can be sung simultaneously because they share the same harmonic structure. Sometimes one of the partner songs works well for recorder.

A great example of partner songs is "One Bottle of Pop." This song consists of three parts, each of which is a song in itself. When the class can sing the whole song independently, divide them into three groups. Perform the song in the manner of a round. When the first group finishes the first part, the second group begins the first part, and so forth. Students can play the first part of the song on their recorders. They can sing the other two parts.

Two songs that work well together in minor tonality are "Hey, Ho, Nobody Home," and "Zum Gali Gali." In order to perform them together, use a combination of playing and singing. In the key of F minor, recorder players can play measure two of "Zum Gali Gali" as an ostinato, while singers perform the songs as partner songs. In the key of G minor, recorder players can perform the first phrase of "Hey, Ho, Nobody Home" as an ostinato while the singers perform the songs as partner songs.

"This Train" and "I'm Ridin' On That New River Train" are two partner songs that can be sung in the key of F. Play the first phrase and last phrase of "This Train" on the recorder, and sing the rest of the song. In "I'm Ridin' On That New River Train," play the first two phrases and sing the rest.

Sometimes it works well to sing a song, then play it on recorder, then sing it again, or sing a different verse. Short songs work well for this sequence. "Amigos," (Tucker, 1985) holds many possibilities. The song is basically a descending C Major scale, so use a sustained C major scale as a warm-up. Students will easily recognize and learn to play the pattern of notes. Students can finger the notes with their recorders in chin position while they sing the words.

Play classroom instruments

Many of the songs on our list are rounds which work well when adding classroom instruments. They are harmonically predictable, repetitive, and lend themselves to creating simple accompaniments. Start with simple borduns on xylophones or metalophones and expand the instrumentation as your students are able. Gradually layer the accompaniment with one or two instruments per lesson over several weeks. Repetition is our friend!

Many rounds are great examples of songs that work well with layering parts. First, everyone learns to sing the song independently. They also learn to sing the song in a four-part round. Learn phrases two, three, and four of the round by rote on recorders. Perform as a round, with each group singing phrase one and playing the other phrases on their recorders. Now students can substitute other instruments for some of the recorder parts. For example, phrase two might be played on xylophones, phrase three on recorders, and phrase four on metallophones. Layer these together gradually. An advanced student might be able to play a more difficult phrase on a chromatic bell set or a chromatic glockenspiel.

Move

It is not safe to move with a recorder in one's mouth! The students playing recorders need to be sitting down, but others who aren't playing can be moving. They may move to a folk dance, or they may create movement to accompany a song. Rounds and short songs with many verses are great for this activity.

Some examples are:
"Rattlin' Bog"
"Alabama Gal"
"Charlie Over the Ocean"

Listen and play

Play the theme of an instrumental piece. Use a CD recording if the key works for recorder. If a CD recording is not in a key that children can manage with ease on the recorder, explain to them that they will play the song in a key that is different from that of the recording. The following pieces have themes that can be learned by rote:

The Nutcracker Suite:
March—key of G;
Coffee—A minor (pitches—G-E-G-E-G-F-G-F-E)
Beethoven's Ninth Symphony: Ode to Joy—key of G
Dvorak's New World Symphony: Theme—key of G or F

Work with rhythm patterns

Begin with four-beat rhythm patterns composed of eighth-note pairs and quarter notes. Play these patterns by rote for children to echo on their recorders, using pitches they have already learned. This can be as simple as using B alone, then A alone, then combinations of Bs and As. Here are some examples of patterns:

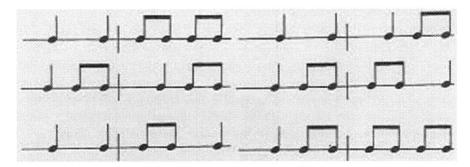

Students can work together in pairs. They can take turns creating four-beat patterns for their partner to echo. Then, allow students to volunteer to lead the class in this same exercise, using patterns that they know or that they create. Add the pitch G when students are ready. Add more pitches as students are able to use these pitches automatically. After B, A, and G, we like to add lower D and E to form the G pentachord. These pitches lend themselves easily to improvisations.

Create by rote

You have been modeling how to create patterns. When students are comfortable creating four-beat patterns using the pitches B, A and G, the pattern echo activity can lead to question/answer improvisation. Choose a student who is adept at creating echo patterns using B, A, and G. Let that student create a four-beat pattern ending on B or A. You then create a four-beat answer ending on G. Tell the children that the pattern that ends on B or A is called a "question phrase." The pattern that ends on G is called an "answer phrase." Ask for more volunteers to play a question phrase for you to answer. Then, ask for volunteers to play an answer for a question phrase that you play. Divide students into pairs to practice question and answer phrases with each other.

Eventually, you can ask the students to compare and contrast your answers and their questions. If you have included some melodic or rhythmic material from the question phrase in your answer, they will be able to hear similarities. Allow the students to practice answering questions with each other using similar melodic and rhythmic material.

Combine activities

Some song material lends itself to a combination of activities, added slowly over a period of time. This process of adding layers is like building a snowball. Make sure each layer is well packed before adding the next layer, or your snowball will fall apart!

The Rally Song (Turkish) is an example of this type of song. After the children learn to sing the song independently, teach them to sing in two parts, with one group chanting the first phrase on D while the rest sing the other two phrases. The children can then learn to sing the whole song as a round. Add the recorder on phrase II as an ostinato. Add a hand drum rhythm pattern throughout, perhaps playing on the steady beat for the first 6 beats of each phrase. If students can add eighth notes, the rhythm pattern could be the same as the second phrase. Add finger cymbals on the 7th beat of each phrase.

Make up a circle dance using grapevine steps, going in and out, turning with finger snaps, and anything else that fits. Children could make up the dance. Three groups of children could each make up a movement for their own phrase. After all have learned the dance, some can dance while some play and sing.

Debka Hora (Israel)

This song is a beautiful round. Part II can start on measure five. Measures five through eight can be the recorder ostinato. Add hand drum, tambourine, and finger cymbal on simple patterns. Add a hora. Some children can play while others dance.

Banuua (Africa)

Teach the song until students can sing it independently. They can then sing it as a round. This song is great for layering. Children can learn the entire song or parts of the song on recorder. Children can extract phrases of the song to make an ostinato for recorders and other instruments, such as xylophones. Students can create accompaniment patterns on drums and various African percussion instruments. They can divide into groups and create movement.

Literacy

Rote playing leads to literacy. Literacy is built on a foundation of rote playing. When students can play many songs and fragments of songs from rote, they have developed the language of music and are ready to read, write, and compose using notation. In our next chapter, we will discuss literacy.

CHAPTER NINE

Literacy

Parallel to the learning of recorder songs by rote, students can be learning to read and write music. Conversational Solfege, by John Feierabend (2001) is an excellent method for pursuing literacy. Through his 12-step method, students progress from rote singing and rhythmic chanting through reading, writing, and creating music. According to Feierabend, students need to "develop skill with patterns before songs" (p. TM15). Since most recorder music books do not provide for this need, you will have to make sure your students master patterns that will be used in songs they are going to play. Students need to learn patterns by rote singing, by reading, and then by writing.

The previous chapters emphasized rote playing, which is the foundation for literacy. This chapter emphasizes reading and composing. Literacy is a stated goal in the National Standards. Recorder playing, while not a tool for reading and composing, can extend those skills.

Reading

When students have mastered patterns and are ready to read recorder music, the following steps work well:

1. Clap the rhythm of the song, speaking rhythm syllables.

2. Sing the pitches of the song using melodic syllables, such as solfege, or letter names, in the correct rhythm. If you work with Curwen hand signs, these may be used at this time.

3. Sing and finger the pitches at the same time, using melodic syllables, in the correct rhythm, with recorder in chin position.

4. Tongue the pitches, softly, and finger at the same time.

5. Think the song and finger at the same time

6. Play!

You may want to make a poster showing the above steps for the students to follow.

What songs are the best ones for beginning readers? The easiest pitches to finger are B, A, and G. Therefore, the best songs with which to begin contain those pitches. We like to add low E as the next pitch. There are a number of songs that include these pitches.

Where do music teachers find songs for their students to read? Your own music series books are a wonderful source of songs. We found that the second grade books contained many playable songs for third graders. The third grade books contained many playable songs for the fourth graders. An advantage of using the previous year's songs for playing is that the children know how to sing them already.

Some of the book series have recorder supplements that provide not only songs, but descants and Orff arrangements as well. Some other supplements are designated as collections of songs for singing and reading. They can be excellent resources for recorder song reading.

There are many commercial recorder method books on the market. These can work well for you, but beware of the song "dumb-down syndrome." Some songs will contain inaccurate rhythms and/or melodies in order to be more easily playable by beginners. However, children will play the songs as they know them. Develop your students' literacy skills separately before they are required to apply them to recorder playing. The songs can then be presented accurately. The children will already know about dotted quarter notes and eighth notes before they learn to play "Mary Had a Little Lamb" and "Jingle Bells" on the recorder!

We developed our own criteria for choosing recorder materials for our classrooms. When we look for recorder books for students to use for reading, we consider a number of questions:

- Is the progression of difficulty gentle enough? Students need much practice with each combination of pitches.
- Are known songs melodically and rhythmically accurate?
- Are meters correct?
- In what order are the pitches introduced? If you are using German recorders, then F can be introduced earlier than for Baroque recorders.

If a CD accompaniment is available:

- Does the instrumentation sound pleasing?
- Are tempos appropriate for beginners?
- Is the harmony correct?

As your students progress in their recorder music reading skills, diversity will inevitably arise. Some students will be ready to read many notes, while others will still be trying to discern B from A. The skill level of most students will fall between the two extremes. We found that by fifth grade, some highly skilled students were feeling bored with whole group reading instruction. Some students were dismally frustrated. Most of the rest were comfortable with the class level of music reading. We decided to differentiate music-reading instruction.

We tested the students, using a song they had been practicing. We then divided them into small groups and devised plans for teaching reading skills to each group. Parent volunteers helped things go more smoothly by working directly with some of the less independent students, and by circulating among all of the groups. Here are some of our suggestions for designing instruction for diverse groups of learners:

- Use large zip-lock bags to organize materials.
- Have a large variety of music available at different skill levels.
- Use music that has CD accompaniments.
- Use CD players with headsets so that students can listen to accompaniments and play along.
- Allow some groups to choose their music from a bin or file of music at or just above their skill level.
- Develop a routine which includes direct instruction followed by independent practice in groups, pairs, or individually.
- Culminate the class with a performance by the various groups, sharing what they learned that day.
- Keep in mind that these reading activities are not the daily focus in music. They are an occasional activity meant to enhance the reading skills of your students. Continue rote playing! Rote playing can be a continuing source of great enjoyment and learning for all of your students.

Composing

Students will learn to write music as part of their regular music literacy studies. They may enjoy composing music specifically for recorder playing. They could write down question and answer phrases they improvise on their recorders and then edit them. There is an advantage to writing down the improvisations: once written, the composer refines the piece, thereby turning an improvisation into a composition.

Question/answer improvisations can become compositions. Give the students a "bank" of pitches from which to choose. Early compositions may have B, A, and G in the bank of possible pitches. This can be expanded to include the members of the G pentachord. Any pitches the students are learning may be added to the bank.

Body percussion rondos make great starters for compositions. Create A, B, and C sections. Each one should have about four measures of a rhythm pattern that uses any or all of these motions: stamp, patsch, clap, fingersnap. Each section should be distinct, so that students can remember them. The *Body Rondo Book* (Solomon, 1990) is a great resource for body percussion rondos.

After students learn the body percussion rondo and can perform it independently, they can use the rhythm patterns to construct a recorder melody. Designate a bank of notes for each section of the rondo. Sections can contrast between major and minor.

Changing the pitches of known songs while keeping the rhythm is another way to compose. For example, "Hop Old Squirrel" can contain low E and D in addition to B, A, and G.

Ideas for reading and composing can be as expansive as your imagination. Have fun! You only need a few more tools in your toolbox to teach recorder successfully. No instructional program is complete without assessment and evaluation. The next chapter will address these important components of teaching and learning.

CHAPTER TEN

Assessment and Evaluation

Assessment is an important part of the educational process. Teachers need feedback to evaluate their students' progress. Students need feedback to evaluate their own progress. Schools and parents expect reports on student progress.

Clearly stated objectives give us something concrete to assess. If your main focus for the recorder lesson is tonguing, then state your objective in terms of what students will be able to do with tonguing by the end of the lesson. For example, "Students will be able to tongue four quarter notes on the pitch B." All of the recorder skills you are teaching can be stated in terms of objectives.

You will decide what level of achievement is acceptable before you move on to another objective. You may set a goal of 90% achievement. This means that 90% of the class will be able to tongue four quarter notes on the pitch B. Some children will continue improving, even though they did not perfectly achieve the objective that day. Perhaps the next day they will be able to demonstrate tonguing. You can leave their grade blank until they achieve an objective, or you can replace their grade with a better one when they achieve the objective.

How can music teachers assess accurately and quickly? Rubrics help teachers and students with assessment by setting up specific criteria for mastery. Three-point rubrics are the quickest to use. As your students take turns demonstrating the skill, listen for accuracy. You can use the following scale for any skill:

      3 points: Consistently accurate/Outstanding

      2 points: Inconsistently accurate/Satisfactory

      1 point: No accuracy/Unsatisfactory

Instead of using points, you could assign a letter grade to each level of skill attainment, depending on the system your school district uses for grading.

Keep assessment sessions as short as possible. Just go down each row quickly, with each student demonstrating the skill as briefly as possible. Enter scores onto your seating chart or directly into your grade book.

Remember, assessment is your friend!

CONCLUSION

We have taken you from rote to write. We have taken you from sound to substance. We hope that while teaching recorder you will share our enthusiasm for and enjoyment of this beautiful instrument.

APPENDIX A

Songs

Use the following table to locate songs for your use in class:

Song	Book	Grade	Page	Other Resources/comments
Alabama Gal				
All Night, All Day				
Angel Band				
Ahrirang				
Banuua				
Bow, Wow, Wow				
Canoe Song				
Charlie Over the Ocean				
Christmas is Coming				
Closet Key				*Conversational Solfege,* J. Feierabend
Come and Sing Together				
Ezekiel Saw the Wheel				
Fais Do Do				Share The Music: *Songs to Sing and Read*
Frere Jacques				
Frog in the Meadow				*Music for Little People,* J. Feierabend
Good News				
Great Big Stars				
Head and Shoulders, Baby				
Hey, Ho, Nobody Home				*Sing and Shine On,* Nick Page
Hinay Mah Tov				Share The Music: *Songs to Sing and Read*
Hot Cross Buns				
I Got a Robe				
I Love the Mountains				
Indian Game Song (Uni Nuni)				*Sing up the Corn, Dance Down the Rain,* Millie Burnett
John the Rabbit				
Kookaburra				
Little David				
Little Tommy Tinker				
Mr. Frog Went A-Courtin'				

Song	Book	Grade	Page	Other Resources/comments
New River Train				STM: *Songs to Sing and Read*
Night Herding Song				STM: *Songs to Sing and Read*
Oh My, No More Pie				*Music for Little People*, J. Feierabend
Oh Won't You Sit Down				
Oh, How Lovely				*Conversational Solfege*, J. Feierabend
Old Brass Wagon				
Old Dan Tucker				
Old MacDonald				
Old Texas				
One Bottle of Pop				
Over My Head				*Sing and Shine On*, Nick Page
Rattlin' Bog				
Row, Row, Row Your Boat				
Sailing at High Tide				
Sandy McNab				STM: *Songs to Sing and Read*
Scotland's Burning				
Seminole Duck Dance				
Sing Together				STM: Songs to Sing and Read
Skin and Bones				
Snail, Snail				*Conversational Solfege*, J.Feierabend.
Sourwood Mountain				
Swapping Song				
Sweetly Sings the Donkey				
Swing Low, Sweet Chariot				
The Clock				Rounds and Canons, Harry Robert Wilson (Pub. Hall & McCreary Co., 1943)
The Fishpole Song				
The Lone Star Trail				
The Orchestra				
There She Goes				*Conversational Solfege*, J. Feierabend
This Little Light				
This Train				
Three Blind Mice				
Trot, Old Joe				
Turkey Song				*Folk Songs, Singing Games, and Play Parties, Vol. 1*, Jill Trinka
Turkish Rally Song				*Ditty Bag*, Janet E. Tobitt
Turn the Glasses Over				
Wayfaring Stranger				
What Kind of Shoes				Silver Burdett 1978 "Centennial" Gr 2
White Sand and Gray Sand				*Book of Rounds*, J. Feierabend
Who Has the Penny?				

APPENDIX B

Chants

"*Tramp, Tramp to Boston*", as collected from family tradition by Norma Kelsey.

Chant while bouncing child or stuffed animal on your knees, facing you. On the word "in," rock forward and pretend to drop child between you knees.

Tramp, Tramp to Boston,
Tramp, Tramp to Lynn,
Look out, little David,
Or you'll fall in!

Five Little Monkeys Jumping on the Bed
Five Little Monkeys Hanging from the Tree
I Have a Little Turtle
Peas Porridge Hot
Patty Cake
Shoe a Little Horse
Whoops Johnny!
Two Little Eyes
Tramp, Tramp to Boston

Resources for Chants:

Book of Fingerplays and Action Songs
John Feierabend
GIA Publications

Books by Helen Wyzga
WWW.Pentatonika.com

APPENDIX C

Sample Letter to Parents

Dear Parents of Third Grade Students,

As part of their music curriculum, boys and girls in the third, fourth, and fifth grades learn to play the recorder. Third graders will begin using recorders during the week of February 2nd.

For health reasons, it's important that each child have his/her own instrument. Any morning next week, your child can purchase a new Aulos brand, one-piece, German style recorder in the school lobby between 8:30 and 9 a.m., for $6.75. This musical instrument will be used for three years or more. Your child may bring cash or a check made out to the Glade Elementary School P.T.A. for that amount.

When your child purchases a recorder, a P.T.A. volunteer will write his/her name on the plastic case and put it in a container that will be stored and locked in the music room. Each time your child's class comes to music, the recorders will be distributed to their owners.

It is important that all the recorders are of the same brand, so that they have the same tone quality and pitch. If you wish to purchase a recorder for your child, please be sure to purchase an Aulos brand one-piece, German-style recorder from a music store, *not* a toy from a toy store or dollar store. If you already have a recorder of the designated brand and style in your home that is not being used, your third-grader can use that instrument for music class. For health reasons, we cannot allow siblings in our school to share the same instrument.

Thank you for supporting your child's music program.

Sincerely,

Ms._____
Music Teacher

RESOURCES

"Amigos"
Judith Cook Tucker
World Music Press (Multicultural Materials for Educators)
PO Box 2565
Danbury CT 06813
WWW.Worldmusicpress.com

Literacy:
Conversational Solfege
John M. Feierabend
GIA Publications, Inc.
7404 South Mason Avenue
Chicago, Illinois 60638

Dance songs recorders can play along with:
"Christy Lane's Complete Party Dance Music" CD
"Christy Lane's Complete Guide to Party Dances" VHS
Distributed by Let's Do It! Pub.
255 N. El Cielo Rd., Ste. 366
Palm Springs, CA 92262

Resources for creating:
The Body Rondo Book [12 body percussion rondos, elementary to advanced]
Jim Solomon
Comprehensive Music Services, Inc.
23123 SW 58th Ave.
Boca Raton, FL 33428-2036

Song collections:
Folk Songs, Singing Games and Play Parties
Jill Trinka
http://www.stthomas.edu/musiced/
University of St. Thomas
St. Paul, Minnesota

Songs for Little People
John Feierabend
GIA Pub.

Rounds and Canons
Arranged and edited by Harry Robert Wilson
Hall & McCreary (1943)

The Ditty Bag
Janet E. Tobitt
Pleasantville, NY

Dance Down the Rain, Sing Up the Corn
Millie Burnett
Musik Innovations
Box 1
Allison Park, PA 15101

Guide to Group Singing:
Sing and Shine On!
Nick Page
World Music Press
www.worldmusicpress.com

REFERENCES

Suzuki, S. (1969). *Nurtured by love: A new approach to education.* New York: Exposition Press.

Suzuki, S., Mills, E., et al. (1973). *The Suzuki concept.* Berkeley: Diablo Press.

Blakeslee, M., ed. (1994). *National standards for arts education.* Reston, VA: Music Educators National Conference.

Feierabend, J. (2001). *Conversational solfege.* Chicago: GIA Publications.

Fritz, R. (2003). *Your Life as Art.* Vermont: Newfane Press.

BIOGRAPHIES

Margo Hall currently teaches general/vocal music at a primary school in Maryland. She holds degrees from The Ohio State University, McDaniel College (formerly Western Maryland) and is a PhD candidate in music education at The University of Maryland. In addition, she completed coursework at Indiana University iof Pennsylvania, Rollins College, and Duquesne. Margo's twenty-seven years of teaching experience in Ohio, Florida and Maryland encompass elementary general vocal music, junior high and middle school general and choral music, and music fundamentals at the college level. She has taught adult guitar classes and piano, directed church choirs, and served as a community children's chorus director. She co-founded the fifth grade honors chorus in her county, still going strong since 1985. Further, she taught action research techniques to music teachers in Lithuania through the APPLE organization and led other teachers in several grant-funded action research projects focused on recorder instruction.

In 1994, Margo received the Charles E. Tressler "Distinguished Teacher Award" for the Frederick County Public Schools. She has led teachers in numerous workshops in Maryland, Pennsylvania and West Virginia. In addition to teaching music, Margo is a certified instructor for a Robert Fritz course entitled, "Creating Your Life."

Norma Kelsey is currently retired from public school teaching. She holds degrees from the University of Massachusetts, Amherst, and Southern Illinois University, where she studied Kodaly methodology with Dorothy Tulloss. In addition, she completed coursework at Penn State University, Duquesne, University of Maryland, Towson, and Hartt. Norma taught elementary general/vocal music for her entire teaching career of over thirty years. Of the many workshops, conventions and courses in which she participated, she was especially influenced by John Feierabend's "Music for Early Childhood" at the Hartt School of Music.

A few years ago, Norma was one of a small group of music teachers who, led by Margo Hall, conducted classroom research on teaching recorders to elementary school children. Together, she and Margo have been presenters for numerous workshops on playing, teaching and learning recorder in Maryland, Pennsylvania and West Virginia.

For several years Norma was a mentor for new music teachers, and she was a co-founder, in 1985, of the now-annual county fifth grade honors chorus. She also served on school district curriculum writing committees.

Norma is a member of a flute choir and occasionally performs in a duo with her husband Morrie, a jazz pianist. Additionally, she is a certified instructor for a Robert Fritz course entitled, "Creating Your Life."

978-0-595-36743-6
0-595-36743-7

504, 510, 518, 521
(3)   (2)   (2)   (2)

519
533
610

533   650   680
(3)   (2)   (1)

544
(3)

649
(3)

9 780595 367436